INNER AFFIRMATIONS

INNER AFFIRMATIONS

USING MINDFULNESS TO CONNECT TO YOUR INNER WISDOM

Katharine A. Chestnut

LNAL Life LLC

Copyright © 2021 by LNAL Life LLC
Atlanta, Georgia

No part of this publication may be reproduced, stored in a retrieval system, or transmitted in any form or by any means, electronic, mechanical, photocopying, recording, scanning, or otherwise, except as permitted under Sections 107 or 108 of the 1976 United States Copyright Act, without the prior written permission of the Publisher. Requests to the Publisher for permission should be addressed to the Permissions Department, LNAL Life LLC, 691 John Wesley Dobbs Avenue, NE, Suite V150, Atlanta, GA 30312.

Limit of Liability/Disclaimer of Warranty: The Publisher and the author make no representations or warranties with respect to the accuracy or completeness of the contents of this work and specifically disclaim all warranties, including without limitation warranties of fitness for a particular purpose. No warranty may be created or extended by sales or promotional materials. The advice and strategies contained herein may not be suitable for every situation. This work is sold with the understanding that the Publisher is not engaged in rendering medical, legal, or other professional advice or services. If professional assistance is required, the services of a competent professional person should be sought. Neither the Publisher nor the author shall be liable for damages arising herefrom. The fact that an individual, organization, or website is referred to in the work as a citation and/or potential source of further information does not mean that the author or the Publisher endorses the information the individual, organization, or website may provide or recommendations they/it may make. Further, readers should be aware that websites listed in this work may have changed or disappeared between when this work was written and when it is read.

For general information on our other products and services or to obtain technical support, please contact our Customer Care Department at customercare@katharinechestnut.com.

LNAL Life LLC publishes its books in a variety of electronic and print formations. Some content that appears in print may not be available in the electronic books, and vice versa.

TRADEMARKS: LNAL Life LLC and the Katharine Chestnut logo are trademarks in the United States and other countries and may not be used without written permission. All other trademarks are the property of their respective owners. LNAL Life LLC is not associated with any product or vendor mentioned in this book.

Interior and Cover Designer:
Danna Mathias of Dearly Creative LLC

Paperback ISBN: 978-1-7376637-0-6
eBook ISBN: 978-1-7376637-2-0

Dedication

To my daughter, Asha

CONTENTS

Introduction	1
How To Use This Book	7
All About Affirmations	11
Non-Dominant Handwriting	19
Creating Your Ritual Of Writing	25
Carry The Message With You	34
Inner Affirmations: Bring On The Benefits!	40
How To Use This Method for #allthethings	47
Inner Wisdom Encouragement	52
Resources For Your Mindfulness Journey	57

Introduction

I woke up in the hospital on Thanksgiving morning in 2017.

I had no idea how I'd gotten there.

Well, I knew *logically* why I wound up in the psychiatric ward the night before. It's because I'd been heading for rock bottom and made a slight detour. But I still wondered that morning, once my brain shifted into gear, how the hell I'd come to this *place*.

And I wondered how I'd get myself OUT of this place.

I knew one thing, deep down: I had to start helping myself. Yes, I'd been in couples and individual therapy for years. I was maintaining certain aspects of life pretty successfully, even holding several jobs at once.

I'd also been crying everyday, more than once a day, for the prior six years. I was so tense and wound so tightly out of fear, that I dreaded the question "How are you?". I knew I would completely break down in front of the person asking the question. I avoided my family and friends.

I had to get out of the hole I was in. But HOW? (I wasn't even sure how I'd gotten here, after all.)

Before panic started to set in, I felt the slightest sense of relief when I suddenly realized: I already had a powerful tool at my fingertips. I found some paper and managed to get a pen.

And I started writing.

"Tears are words that need to be written."
— Paulo Coelho

This book, *Inner Affirmations*, has been in the works for more than a decade now. After many friends (and my therapist) encouraged me, I knew it was time to write and publish the damn thing.

Inner Affirmations didn't start out as an idea for a book, or even a full idea.

It started when I set out to heal my self-doubt.

I never doubted my business abilities. When it came to my career, I had excelled and advanced at whatever I put my mind to do. I was sure of my skills, and my ability to learn new ones.

The thing was, deep down, I doubted my ability to trust myself — specifically, when something didn't feel right. So many times in my personal life, there was a little whisper inside of me. It kept me alert and on edge. I started to live with the sense that there was something off. Instead of addressing my discomfort in the situation or the relationship, I wondered what was bothering me so much. And promptly shrugged it off.

I didn't listen to those whispers.

This distrust of my instincts attracted those who could sense and exploit my weakness. It's how I found myself in a mentally, emotionally and sexually abusive marriage to a covert narcissist for over a decade. I became overwhelmed by self-doubt and filled with shame as my situation grew more and more dire over the years. Too often, I reasoned my way out of my fears. I'd completely stopped listening to my own instincts.

I was drowning in this self-doubt. It weighed me down and made me feel trapped. I did remember my journaling habit at times. I had created and used a specific method for writing, that I later called my "Inner Affirmations" method. It was always present in the back of my mind. I still knew its structure and ritual. Along with its value.

But during this marriage, I hadn't really used my process for journaling — my spouse mocked it as illogical and "New Age."

So my journaling habit went on the back burner for a while. For more than a few years, actually.

HOW TO SAVE YOURSELF: INNER AFFIRMATIONS

Even when I was tense and full of fear in my abusive relationship, the gift of my inner wisdom was still real to me. I had discovered how to access my wisdom without doubts or second-guessing, and although I had stopped journaling regularly, I could still connect with that source of self-empowered wisdom when I felt strong enough to listen.

Eventually, the abuse in the relationship started to take its toll. The lows got incredibly low and dark, to the point of devastation.

So when I woke up in the psychiatric unit that day in 2017, I realized I needed to address the hurt I'd been going through. This was my wake up call.

The first thing I did when I started the process of recovery (and separation from my now ex), was to pull out my trusty (albeit dusty) journal. **This is when I started the work of saving my own life.**

I was exhausted though. It felt like a physical struggle, as if I'd actually been swimming in mud. On very rare occasions, several years later, I still feel like that. But my healing started when I pulled out my journal. I began using my Inner Affirmations method again. I made a ritual out of it, which you'll read more about in the coming chapters.

Six months into my healing, I came across Melanie Tonia Evans and the Narcissistic Abuse Recovery Program (NARP).[1] NARP gave me the guidance and structure (which my logical and pragmatic side adored) to start working through and releasing my experience of trauma.

I also started meditating during this period of healing. I had never been able to quiet or calm my mind successfully in the past. Then I found Insight Timer[2], which hosts the largest collection of free meditations online. Here, I discovered the concept of guided meditation. It was exactly what I needed to slow down and feel grateful for all my experiences. I exhausted the app's sessions geared toward narcissistic abuse recovery. (Eventually, I decided to make my own and now have an extensive library of guided meditations on many topics[3]).

As I healed, I noticed my Inner Affirmations journaling starting to shift. My ability to forgive myself progressed in stages. The healing process was not linear — I would regularly move forward three steps only to fall back two. Eventually, I came to a place of forgiveness and compassion for my former abuser as well as my contribution in the experience.

I had tucked the idea of Inner Affirmations away, knowing it was something that I would share someday. Even if only one person found relief by accessing their inner wisdom with this method, I knew I had to put it out there as an example.

This is just one way to heal. But it's what has worked for me.

WHY THIS WORKS

We all have a transformative power at our fingertips. The process I developed for myself came through the exercise of trial and error — and eventually, I discovered my way closer to inner peace and wisdom.

What I've learned is that when I start to listen and then trust that message, I am able to harness a creative and nurturing force. One that is powerful enough to help me work through every challenge and obstacle.

This force is inside us all the time. You might call that force empowerment or divinity or a Higher Self. But only when we learn to **trust that force** — to trust ourselves and our experiences — will it start to work.

I want you to be able to reconnect with your inner wisdom like I did. I know that everyone is capable of harnessing their own powerful inner wisdom. I'm finally in a place where I feel safe to communicate this practice with people who might need it. I know that my vulnerability will allow readers to experience similar profound effects so that they, too, are open to its transformation.

After reading this book and learning the *Inner Affirmations* method, you'll be able to write your own affirmations — affirmations that are perfectly suited to you in the moment.

Affirmations that will gently nudge you toward a deeper understanding of yourself and your place in the universe.

Sources:
1. *Melanie Tonia Evans, Narcissistic Abuse Recovery Program (NARP)*
2. *Insight Timer*
3. *Insight Timer - Katharine A. Chestnut*

How to Use This Book

This book isn't about quick fixes or magic spells. It's not something you'll consume or assimilate in one weekend.

In fact, this book isn't about reading — it's about writing. It's about learning to develop a habit that will support your growth, and it's about cultivating a more sustainable journaling practice. It's a journaling habit that I think, and sincerely hope, you'll stick with.

This book is about lasting, healing change over the course of your life. Together, we're going to make gradual changes and adjustments in your daily routine. By making these changes slowly, you have a better chance of filling the gap between where you are now and where you want to be in your new journaling practice.

WHAT ARE INNER AFFIRMATIONS?

As a girl, I was fortunate to be introduced to traditional and alternative religions along with spiritual perspectives — from religions like Catholicism and Hare Krishna to philosophies like Buddhism and even witchcraft.

I had no idea that these varied experiences during my youth would help me to make sense of life and significant events in later years. Having some introduction to differing philosophies, I was open to learning more and discovering my own spirituality.

I cannot take credit for my introduction to a deeper connection through my writing. More than 20 years ago, I was personally introduced to and worked with the late Sue Myers, a million-dollar-club realtor turned spiritual guide. She guided me to find a path that resonated with me. In the end, I found *my own* spirituality, and it has helped me to navigate relationships, develop my values, and seek my life's purpose.

Sue's reasoning and no-nonsense approach appealed to my strong sense of logic. She introduced me to the concept of non-dominant handwriting. By practicing this method, I found that my writing voice was far more authentic. I was able to get out of my head and focus on what I knew to be true **in my body**, just by writing with my non-dominant hand.

I was writing without getting in my own way.

Inner Affirmations is a guide to getting out of your own way and connecting with a powerful source of loving, affirmative energy. That energy is already inside of you — it's inside **all of us**.

This book is a guide for anyone who wants to develop a practice of mindfulness. "Mindfulness" is frequently considered a buzzword these days, but this journaling practice isn't just about filling pages. It's really about being open to listening.

I want this practice to stick with you. Each of the steps you'll take during your writing ritual in the chapters are intended to help create that sticky-ness, so that you really do keep up with the habit.

When you start to develop a regular journaling practice in the way I'm recommending, you'll have a source of healing at your fingertips all the time.

If you're open to it, that is.

So often we lose touch with ourselves and the transformative power that lives within us. Our Western culture values rationalism; this is instilled in us from birth. And while scrambling to keep up with daily schedules, experiencing loss, or healing from devastating relationships — all of these things make it easy to forget just how amazing and resilient the human spirit can be.

This book is a way to share with you the best, most accessible, most efficient way to access your own limitless and transformative power.

You'll want to have a journal, notebook, or just a pad of paper on hand. When I started, I had an old, partially used composition book. After filling that up, I moved to a spiral notebook. Once while traveling, I brought a beautiful blue leather notebook in an airport. It was lovely — and I found myself not writing as much since I wanted to savor it. I finally landed on a smaller, bound notebook that suited me better and that I didn't mind filling up as I needed. You can find plenty online (my favorites are in the Resources section of this book). Whatever you use, never forget that it is about the writing more than the tools.

I sincerely wish for you to find your inner voice and the affirmations that are inside of you. I know those words will give you strength and hope when you need it most.

Thank you for being open, and for trusting me to guide you on that journey.

CHAPTER 1
All About Affirmations

"Your best is going to change from moment to moment; it will be different when you are healthy as opposed to sick. Under any circumstance, simply do your best, and you will avoid self-judgment, self-abuse and regret."
—Don Miguel Ruiz

When you hear the word "affirmation," concepts like self-empowerment and positive thinking probably come to mind. Wikipedia[1] suggests that "an affirmation is a statement that is repeated and written down frequently."

Affirmations, to put it simply, are statements of belief.

Affirmations have been used throughout history, in prayers and rituals found in different cultures. In 1910, Wallace D. Wattles helped to popularize the use of affirmations in his book *The Science of Getting Rich*[2]. The book was successful at the time — it's still in print today because of its widespread influence on spiritual movements, books like *The Secret*[3], and other schools of thought.

Wattles developed a "Certain Way of Thinking," which included using self-affirmations to create a state of mental positivity. And what he and countless others have found is that repeated positive statements have a (sometimes surprising) influence on underlying negative beliefs.

Throughout the years, people have transformed their mindset by replacing cynical thoughts with more constructive statements of belief. Those who wanted to overcome self-sabotage and a pessimistic outlook on life saw improvement when they used affirmations.

Affirmative statements encourage us — they can help to anchor us in times of struggle or extreme anxiety. People use affirmations for all sorts of reasons, but with one consistent goal: to create a reality that's happier, more fulfilling, and more successful than what we've previously believed to be possible.

Millions have been using affirmations to think more positively since the 1910s. Affirmation statements are found frequently in self-care practices, social media memes, and modern spirituality.

Affirmations aren't just a trend. And research shows us that they're highly effective when approached the right way.

Pause a moment before you move on to consider:
- Why did you buy this book?
- What did you hope to learn?

WHY AFFIRMATIONS?

According to psychiatrist and author Dr. Walter E. Jacobson, what we believe about ourselves at a subconscious level can have a significant impact on the outcome of future events in our lives.

In other words, a belief like "I suck at bowling" can actually predict whether or not you're able to knock down any pins.

Affirmations neutralize this negative pattern of thinking — and by focusing on the positive, either by repeating statements or writing them down, you can train your brain out of a toxic and limiting mindset. Refocusing your thoughts this way can have some pretty magical results.

And science backs up this magic. Let's take a look at some studies done in recent years.

In one research study[4], women aged 18–24 were divided into an experimental group and a control group. The experimental group used cognitive behavioral intervention methods over a long-term period. These methods included stopping negative thoughts and using positive affirmations in their daily lives.

The results showed that the individuals in the intervention group experienced higher self-esteem and a decrease in depressive symptoms and negative thinking. Self-affirmation techniques have also been shown to reduce the effects of performance anxiety for test-takers. In 2013, 80 undergraduate students were divided into a control group and an experimental group[5]. The experimental group was directed to use self-affirmation techniques before taking a timed test in front of an evaluator, usually a high-stress situation.

Their results showed that using a self-affirmations technique in this situation acts as a "stress buffer." Individuals in the control group, who didn't use affirmations, performed less favorably than the experimental group, who used self-affirmations during their tests.

The studies performed on affirmations have backed up what scientists learned back in the 1920s — that negative thoughts and limiting beliefs can seriously throw us off our game. Stopping those self-deprecating, invasive thoughts and replacing them with more positive, confidence-building affirmations goes a long way toward success. In fact, by stating affirmations, chronically stressed people can protect themselves from an onslaught of overly anxious thoughts — thoughts that would otherwise sabotage them.

Practicing affirmations even rewires our brains over time. The women in the first study saw long-term success when they kept up the affirmations while the practice continued to help decrease their depression symptoms. If you've struggled through any kind of mental health issue, you know what kind of physical toll that can take on you. That's why affirmations are such a powerful tool: they can help you get your life back.

A really interesting process goes on in our brains when we start using affirmations. Scientists have started looking at those brain mechanics, and they've found (through functional magnetic resonance imaging, or fMRI) that

self-affirmation lights up the reward centers in our brains[6]. The same parts of the brain that react to winning an award or eating dessert get activated when we self-affirm.

The science shows that self-affirmation also increases activity areas of the brain that are connected to self-related processing. When we think and process positive thoughts, these thoughts can act as protection against painful or negative information we might be getting. Affirmations are a great buffer against potentially harmful or scary stimuli that we might encounter.

Because affirmations are so powerful, they should be approached with care: in fact, some types of affirmations can have a detrimental effect on you.

Think about this:
- Do you use or have you used affirmations?

THE TROUBLE WITH TRADITIONAL AFFIRMATIONS

There's been extensive research on affirmations and how much of an impact they can have on our mental health. The results are always significant (at least, I'm impressed) — but some kinds of positive affirmations don't have the kind of impact that we might think.

Behavioral studies have found that saying positive affirmations in the present tense can **actually have a detrimental effect** on people with low self-esteem.

Here's why: Positive affirmations aren't just wishful thinking, as a lot of skeptics have suggested. Just saying positive statements ("I have healthy eating habits") without **truly feeling or believing** them can backfire on you.

Josh Steimle — a highly successful author, speaker, and entrepreneur — has a whole list[7] of reasons why present-tense affirmations like this might not work for people, and he points out that the effectiveness of an affirmation has a lot to do with sincerity.

"The problem with affirming something about yourself is that you're committing yourself to action, and you may not really want to do what you're committing to do, and so you may feel that affirmation is insincere," Josh explains.

Instead, he suggests tricking yourself: "The interesting thing about sincerity is that you can trick yourself into it by wanting to want what you **think** you want."

Using a statement like "I want to have healthier eating habits" is a better way of affirming yourself in that situation. This is a sincere, authentic, from-your-core statement. You might not have "great" eating habits right now, but you truly want to eat healthier.

Affirmations are about your internal power; they represent a kind of self-mastery. Affirmations bring about a keen awareness of your true core values. As social psychologist and Harvard lecturer Amy Cuddy says in her bestseller *Presence*[8], "This is about your unfiltered self; presence is being the person you are in the best moments of your life."

I firmly believe that the biggest problem we all have is getting in our own way, especially when it comes to just being in the present moment. My friends and colleagues can confirm what I've said time and again — that I spend much of my life in my head. I've spent so much time up there in my head that I don't always allow myself to trust what I'm feeling in my gut or what I know to be true deep down in my heart.

After all, logical thinking is much more highly regarded in our society than emotions.

That logical, rational thinking, while motivating me to be successful in business, caused me grief and pain in my personal life. It wasn't until I started to *trust* the emotions I was **feeling** (along with a healthy dose of logic) that I was able to help myself, and reconnect with what I truly value and know to be true.

Affirmations are the path toward living out those values; these are values that you already know in your core. And your most powerful affirmations are already within you — perhaps just not the way you think.

EXERCISE

Before you race to the next chapter, get out your notebook and pen. Take a few minutes to write down the answers to these questions:

- What quality about you is most unique?
- Why do people want you in their lives?
- What quality do others consider to be your strongest asset?
- What quality makes you feel really alive and wonderful when you express it?
- What quality is most evident when you are being the most powerful?

Sources:
1. *Affirmations (New Age). (2021, May 10). In Wikipedia.*
2. *Wallace D. Wattles, (1910) The Science of Getting Rich. JonRose Publishing.*
3. *Rhonda Bryne, (2008) The Secret. Simon & Schuster.*
4. *Peden, A. R., Hall, L. A., Rayens, M. K., and Beebe, L. L. (2001). Preventing Depression in High-Risk College Women: A Report of an 18-Month Follow-Up. Journal of American College Health, 49(6): 299–306.*
5. *Creswell, J. D., Dutcher, J. M., Klein, W. M. P., Harris, P. R., and Levine, J. M. (2013). Self-Affirmation Improves Problem Solving under Stress. PLOS One.*
6. *Cascio, C. N., O'Donnell, M. B, Tinney, F. J., Lieberman, M. D., Taylor, S. E., Strecher, V. J., and Falk, E. B. (2015). Self-affirmation Activates Brain Systems Associated with Self-Related Processing and Reward and is Reinforced by Future Orientation. NCBI.*
7. *Steimle, Josh. 7 Reasons Positive Affirmations Aren't Working for You.*
8. *Cuddy, Amy. (2015). Presence. Little, Brown Spark.*

CHAPTER 2
Non-Dominant Handwriting

> "The art of writing is the art of
> discovering what you believe."
> —*Gustave Flaubert*

Have you ever tried to write with your non-dominant hand? Perhaps you tested this out as a child, wondering what it might feel like to write with your other hand.

You probably remember how it felt, too: frustrating and humbling at the same time, because you weren't able to form letters easily or quickly. It probably felt awkward and wrong.

That is **exactly** what I'm saying to do here. And I hope that you make a regular practice out of it, because of how much value this kind of writing will bring into your life. Non-dominant handwriting has been such a huge part of my own self-growth and a support for my mental health. This practice of writing has strengthened me in many ways I can't even articulate.

It's that powerful.

When you write with your non-dominant hand, you're so focused on forming the letters that the act becomes highly intentional. And that intentionality means your ego can't interfere with the inspiration that is coming in.

That intentionality moves you toward a place of mindfulness.

A place that allows you to get **out** of your head and **into your heart**.

WHY NON-DOMINANT HANDWRITING?

OK, but really? Why non-dominant handwriting? Why focus on this method of journaling when you could write in a more free-flowing way? Why would I write something I can't even read?

There's a place for journaling with your dominant hand, too; don't get me wrong. Sometimes I need to do some stream-of-consciousness writing that spills onto the page without effort.

Non-dominant handwriting is a gift because it supports that journaling practice, too. Non-dominant handwriting boosts your brain activity. If you normally write with your right hand, the left side of the brain controls that activity. When you start using the opposite hand, you activate the other side of the brain. This actually **strengthens the connections** between your two brain hemispheres; essentially, you're having to think extra hard about using a hand that you don't typically use. And overall, you're strengthening brain activity[1] in both sides of your brain. (Everyone wins!)

Non-dominant handwriting means having to think more carefully about each word, even each letter, that you write down. It is an **act of mindfulness**.

"Perhaps the greatest thing about handwriting is that the very act of doing it forces you to focus on what's important. It is, in essence, a moment of mindfulness," according to meditation site Headspace[2].

Non-dominant handwriting forces you to slow down even more and think about each small movement.

And that's where the magic (and science) starts to happen.

Mindfulness is quite the trend these days. Intentionality exercises — anything from breathwork to yoga to meditation — all do a great job of s-l-o-w-i-n-g you down.

In these types of practices, you're forced to focus on just being in your body. Because you get out of your head, away from distracting thoughts and a racing mind, your ego also quiets down and falls away into the background.

This kind of activity allows you to be with your authentic self, without your chattering, demanding ego getting in the way.

You can be fully and wholly in your body because you're activating the parasympathetic system. That's the same part of your nervous system that allows you to calm down and rest, breathe more deeply, and fully digest your food. On the flip side of that is the sympathetic system: the one that activates your "fight, flight, or freeze" response and keeps you alert and anxious.

Because the act of writing with your non-dominant hand activates your parasympathetic system, you're slowing down. By being more fully in your body, you allow a different type of wisdom to shine through while you write.

This is wisdom that comes from your own truth — from your own authentic self.

That's why non-dominant handwriting is also one of the most effective ways of connecting with your spiritual self. Any act of mindfulness, like meditation and non-dominant handwriting, is a highly effective way to communicate with your guides, whether that's God, a Higher Power, your ancestors, or your angels.

Non-dominant handwriting is powerful because it creates the space for this kind of connection and communication. And it creates a foundation for self-affirmation that will support you for the rest of your life, especially if you're practicing it on a regular basis.

Now it's your turn to try it.

LET'S EXPERIMENT

Don't worry if you can't read your handwriting or what it looks like when you try this out. Remember, you are sidestepping your ego. You might even feel your ego fighting this process — the ego loves to be in charge, to control everything perfectly.

Essentially, you're going to focus on being in your body. So let's get started.

- Get paper and a pen. It doesn't matter what kind, and don't overthink it. You're just on a test drive.
- Find a comfortable place to sit that you can write easily. Make sure your legs are uncrossed and your feet are on the floor.
- Get grounded in your body with a short breathing meditation. For at least three minutes, focus on intentional breathing — that means full breaths into your belly and long exhales that let everything go (Check out the Insight Timer app for guided breathing exercises if you need extra help or even use mine).
- Now, write your name with your non-dominant hand.
- Put the pen back in your dominant hand and write, "How did that feel writing with my non-dominant hand?"
- Now, put the pen back in your non-dominant hand and let the answer flow when you write. Was it awkward? Slow? Did you feel silly, stupid, childish? Perhaps you found it fun. Relaxing? Creative? Liberating?

SECOND EXERCISE

Now, let's revisit the questions from the first chapter with your non-dominant hand, without looking at what you wrote the first time you answered the questions.

- What quality about you is most unique?
- Why do people want you in their lives?
- What quality do others consider to be your strongest asset?
- What quality makes you feel really alive and wonderful when you express it?
- What quality is most evident when you are being the most powerful?

If you are like most people, the second sets of answers were different from the first set. They may have similarities, and I'll bet there were a few surprises in there.

RELISH IN THE MAGIC

What surprises did you find?

Did you find that people want you in their lives for different reasons than you initially wrote?

Perhaps your strongest asset is something you don't often think about or admit. These surprise answers are unfiltered messages — they are messages that came from simply being fully in your body.

There is magic in these surprises.

And there's also an immense, powerful amount of self-wisdom that comes from being grounded and mindful, and letting yourself just **be**, instead of second-guessing and editing yourself while you write.

Sources:
1. Gut, Malgorzata, Urbanik, Andrzej, Forsberg, Lars, Binder, Marek, Rymarczyk, Krystyna, Sobiecka, Barbara, Kozub, Justyna, and Brabowska, Anna. (2007). Brain Correlates of Right-Handedness. Acta Neurobiologiae Experimentalis, 67(1): 43–51.
2. Does Writing By Hand Sharpen Your Creativity. Headspace.

CHAPTER 3

Creating Your Ritual of Writing

> "Your daily life is your temple and your religion. When you enter into it, take with you your all."
> —*Khalil Gibran*

Think about a few of the most significant moments in your life — maybe your marriage, a birthday celebration, a relative's funeral, or your graduation.

These impactful events stand out in our memories, and it's often because they're surrounded by ritual.

Rituals can be smaller than a full-blown, day-long event. The rituals of making a morning coffee or taking a relaxing bath, for example, hold a great deal of meaning, even if those situations seem mundane.

Ritual helps us create meaning around an event because of the intention that goes into the ritual. When we surround a seemingly small activity, like a morning coffee or bath, with intentional actions (like carefully pouring water over your favorite coffee grounds, or lighting candles near the tub), these activities start to take on more importance. They become more fulfilling and nourishing to us.

Rituals create sacred space in our daily lives. And we could all use more of that, right?

I have a ritual to start each day. I get up early enough in the morning to have some time to myself. I do this before the demands of my day kick in and my mind starts to wander toward all the things on my schedule.

I sit in a quiet place that I'm comfortable in and start my journaling ritual. While I'm sitting, I start with a meditation and do some breathing exercises to get centered and grounded. It's a necessary part of any ritual: the physical space you're in, including your body, will set the tone for how effective your ritual is.

Once I've gotten more grounded, I start journaling with my non-dominant hand. I write in a special journal, one set aside specifically for my journaling practice.

But what do I write?

JUST WRITE: SOME PROMPTS

Most days, I have no idea what I'm going to write about. So I have a few topics and prompts on hand to get the creative juices flowing. Here are some of them:

Practice Gratitude

Even if I can't think of anything profound, I still write about what I am grateful for in that moment, whether it's the sunshine, a purring cat, the birds chirping, or the crepe myrtles blooming.

The practice of gratitude can be powerful. Many therapists and counselors will recommend that their clients focus on gratitude. Studies have shown time and time again that this practice can yield significant results. In one research study[1] at Berkeley, participants who wrote gratitude letters "reported significantly better mental health for four weeks and again 12 weeks after their writing exercise ended. This suggests that gratitude writing can be beneficial not just for healthy, well-adjusted individuals, but also for those who struggle with mental health concerns."

Ask Myself a Question

Sometimes our heads are full and swirling with thoughts. Maybe it feels impossible to meditate and clear your head. Perhaps something is on your mind, troubling you. Or maybe you woke up knowing you've got a big day ahead.

Step back to notice this activity, to give yourself perspective on these thoughts. Simply write the question, "What is it that I need to know about the situation/day/

etc.?" Don't judge your thoughts; just look at them, observe what's going on, and write.

Pull an Oracle or Tarot Card
I have several sets of oracle cards that I've collected over the years, but my favorite are the *Angel Blessings*[2] cards by Kimberly Marooney. Pulling a card and reading from the accompanying book about its meaning is a great way to prompt my writing. Often there's a message in the cards that assists me in considering a situation differently. Getting this additional perspective is always a benefit.

Or perhaps there is something in the reading that resonates with me and I feel the need to explore it further.

Write a Letter
Sometimes the best way to get the words out on paper is having a person to direct them to. A few of my journal entries are letters to myself, to a Higher Power, or to loved ones. These messages are some of the most revealing (and touching) entries that I've written, and if I'm at a loss for words when I start to journal, I'll often just start a letter.

Meditate on Daily Affirmations
There are loads of sites that offer daily affirmations to visitors. You can visit these sites and meditate on an affirmation posted there, then start writing. I also offer my own inner affirmations daily on my homepage.

My hope is that you'll start to see how you're creating affirmations for yourself. For me, non-dominant handwriting has been a key part of putting those affirmations into words because the process of writing with my "wrong" hand is intentional and mindful.

So how do I create those affirmations? Sometimes I just pick a topic to focus on…

Choose a Topic
My website and social media are filled with many of my own inner affirmations. If you subscribe to my newsletter, you'll know that I've published a companion journal to accompany this book, which includes affirmations that I've written over the years. Because there are so many, I've sorted them into four categories: **Listen, Nurture, Act, and Love.**

- ***Listen**: Listen to your inner wisdom or messages from the Universe.*
- ***Nurture**: Nurture yourself as you are healing and growing.*
- ***Act**: Take action on your messages and what you've learned.*
- ***Love**: Love yourself, the Universe, and everything in it, unconditionally and without judgment.*

I hope these ideas for journaling bring some inspiration and prompt your writing. It's important to remember that no matter how you begin writing, just start putting the words down.

Let your words flow onto the page. Don't think beyond the first question or statement or edit yourself as you go forward.

Just write.

SET ASIDE EXPECTATIONS

There are some mornings when I write one page with my non-dominant hand, and that's all I've got.

Sometimes, I write for pages and pages. I've written blogs and meditations this way — even parts of this book.

I know that there will be something helpful each time I write with my non-dominant hand. It doesn't matter how small it is, as each is a glimpse into my inner wisdom. Sometimes what I write catches me off guard — it's surprising because I have no idea where it comes from.

Then I remember: **It comes from me.** I trust that I hold the truth inside me — and it needs to come out.

You'll need to set aside expectations and judgment first. Yes, this takes practice. It takes an openness. It takes being mindful.

And yes, even after years of practicing this way of journaling, I get stuck in my own head. When I started writing this book, I was focused on the launch date and getting the word out about that, and I'd get trapped in my own marketing mind (my comfort zone). I started focusing on how to craft the words perfectly, or how my affirmations might be perceived on social media. I found myself expecting to have something profound each time I wrote.

That kind of thinking just gets you stuck. **Hint:** There's **not** a perfect way to do this. In fact, it's about fighting against those expectations and the urge to do things a "right" way.

This practice is about letting things flow. The words, or messages, want to come out — you just have to let them.

And you sure as hell can't force that process or fit your affirmations into a nice, Instagrammable message.

So, once you have finished writing for the day, look at what you have written. It may not make sense. It may just be challenging to decipher!

However, I always find a nugget (maybe even just one word or phrase) that jumps out at me. Every time. On occasion, I go back to my old journals — I have quite a few now — and find affirmations in those entries that I may not have wanted to accept in that moment.

I've also used my non-dominant writing practice to help me develop ideas for workshops and other exercises. Sometimes my ego gets in the way of the work I have on my plate. We can all be incredibly critical of ourselves and the work we do. I've found that my practice of non-dominant handwriting is a great way to bypass that kind of judgmental thinking.

I just have to trust the process.
You have to trust the process.

EXERCISE

Set up your space for the ritual of your regular writing practice. This isn't about designing the perfect writing nook, though. It's more about finding the right setting or type of space for your practice. For me, my writing ritual usually happens on my back porch in a cozy chair.

Organize a part of your room or an outdoor area that allows you some alone time. Make sure it's comfortable, free of distraction, and maybe even a little indulgent: Soft pillows, candles with your favorite scent, and good lighting can all help to set the stage. I like to make sure I can nestle somewhere for a little bit while I write. Note: I make it a point not to write at my desk (that's for work) or in bed (that's for sleeping).

You should also find a journal that appeals to you. I get BooQool black hardcover journals from Amazon. It took me a little while to find the right journal for me, though.

It can help to think through some features of journals and notebooks that might sway your purchase:

- If aesthetics are important, you might find a high-end journal that feels really special to you. There are a myriad of ways to personalize your journal's cover.
- There are a few different sizes of notebook to choose from. Want something travel-sized? Need the feel for a bigger page? Think about how and where you might use your journal.
- Are you okay with a simple spiral notebook, or do you prefer a bound version? Sometimes spiral notebooks can get caught on keys and don't always fit in bags well.

- Don't want to use up paper? Consider a reusable notebook — there are a few different versions out there that come with the benefit of saving and organizing your pages digitally.

You might also buy a set of nice pens that you'll enjoy writing with, and there are plenty of options to choose from that will fit your budget. Maybe you don't want to spend too much on something you'll just lose later. But you might still consider what color ink you prefer, or if you'd like a variety of colors to choose from. Some pens offer a smoother transfer of ink and glide easily on the page. Or perhaps you want a fun, quirky pen with aromatic ink or cheery colors.

Think about the experience that you want to create when you're writing, and spend a little time considering the tools you'll be working with.

Then, put your writing practice on your calendar, or set an alarm to give yourself time each day. Whatever you need to prompt you — this ritual is about setting aside time and space for a practice that serves and nourishes you.

I can't wait for you to get started!

Sources:
1. *Brown, Joshua, and Wong, Joel. (2017, June 6). How Gratitude Changes You and Your Brain. Greater Good Magazine.*
2. *Marooney, Kimberly. (2010). The Angel Blessings Kit, Revised Edition: Cards of Sacred Guidance and Inspiration. Fair Winds Press*

CHAPTER 4
Carry the Message with You

> "No one saves us but ourselves. No one can and no one may. We ourselves must walk the path."
> —*Buddha*

YOUR MESSAGE

Have you tried out your writing ritual yet? Hopefully the practice of non-dominant handwriting will start to feel like a natural, mindful, fruitful part of your day.

The next step in this journaling practice is an important one, even if it seems a little mundane:

You're going to start carrying your affirmations with you. Here's how it works:

- Review what you've written that day. Find that one sentence (or maybe two) that really stands out to you.

- Write those words down on a separate slip of paper (using your dominant hand so it is legible) so that the sentence feels like a single, tangible object.
- Take that slip of paper and put it in your pocket or someplace on your person — sometimes I keep mine in the strap of my bra or tank top.

When you go about your day, place your hand on the slip of paper. You can pull it out and read it, or just take a moment to touch it and remember your journaling practice.

The slip of paper is small, but the magic is there. The slip of paper acts as a symbol. It's a tiny love letter to yourself.

And it's a written testament to the wisdom that lives inside of you.

In any case, it's **your** affirmation, and it stays with you to guide you through the day. This small slip of paper **reinforces** your own beautiful and powerful source of wisdom — a reminder that you already have everything you need to be fulfilled.

The power of reinforcement throughout your day isn't something to sneeze at. Like creating a ritual, the act of reinforcement can bring about lasting benefits. The piece of paper is a tactile reinforcer. In other words, it's a physical reminder of your affirmation.

Let's say your day starts to get stressful or weighs you down. Touching your affirmation acts as a kind of self-soothing exercise, a bit like a worry stone.

Neuroscientist and author Dr. Joan C. King used a similar method of reinforcement and kept slips of paper with her favorite quotes written on them. Reading those quotations was a way for her to spend "hidden periods of time."

For example, you might get stuck somewhere like the doctor's office and feel frustrated by the wait. "When I find myself in one of these hidden periods of time, like waiting in line at the bank, I pull out a slip of paper and allow myself to expand into a larger vision by reading the quotation," King writes in her book, *Cellular Wisdom*[1].

Having your own small physical reminder of your affirmation brings you back to the moment you had earlier, when you were connected to your own inner wisdom and writing it down. You'll be reminded of your mindfulness practice. Even in the midst of a busy day, you'll have this affirmation to bring you back to that place of inspiration.

By starting this habit, you're developing a practice to help you cope with stress or other negative triggers during the day. This kind of coping mechanism will create a significant impact in those moments. And when you start to do that more often, these slips of paper bring some big benefits:

- They establish your self-efficacy. Quite simply, that's your own innate knowledge that you can handle what life has thrown at you. All the experiences and challenges you've been through have produced a whole, functioning person. Even if you're going through hell, you've still been able to get to where you are now, despite your "failures" or setbacks. You're alive, and you know how to get through **real** (sometimes really real) life.

- Physically touching the slip of paper reminds you of your grounding, mindful journaling practice. On days when it feels like there's just one disaster after another, touching the slip of paper can trigger positive emotions and self-confidence. You might even be able to breathe a little easier. (In fact, you might try taking a few deep, luxurious breaths any time you touch that piece of paper.)
- Once you do this a few times, you'll be able to start a collection of these pieces of paper. These become reminders — physical proof! — of your new, healthy habit. You can keep these slips of paper, or you might even share them: Tape them to a mirror in a public bathroom, or type up the message and share it with your followers. Spread the love.

In the (very difficult) time in my life when I fell off track with my journaling practice, I bottled things up and let them fester. I was fearful and anxious, bracing myself against more disappointment and heartbreak. Instead of carrying affirmations along with me, I carried self-doubt and toxic thinking.

I don't beat myself up over this. I probably wasn't ready to write about what was going on during this incredibly dark period.

I do feel strongly that some of my health problems at that stage in my life could be attributed to the fact that I wasn't expressing my thoughts or connecting with my body in a mindful way.

What I learned is that when you don't take time to process your days, issues start to pop up. When you meditate on or write about these things, you'll notice if you need to work (or write) through some of your problems so they don't become recurring or disastrous.

That's the beautiful thing about habits — you can always get back on track with them. You can replace an unhealthy habit with a new, more nourishing habit.

Because I started writing again, I now have baskets of love letters to myself.

They're a reminder that I have always held truth and wisdom inside of me, even during the darkest and scariest of times, when I doubted myself and everything I knew. Note: If you want examples of these affirmations, check out katharinechestnut.com or find me on social, where I post affirmations regularly!

These slips of paper are powerful, and I can't wait for you to experience what's in store for you when you cultivate this kind of loving habit in your life.

EXERCISE

By now, you should have practiced some non-dominant handwriting. Maybe you only have a few entries in your journal, and that will work just fine.

- Open your journal and take a look at what you've written recently. Find a few words or sentences that really stand out.
- Write those words down on a separate slip of paper using your dominant hand. It doesn't have to be on fancy paper — some days I use whatever I've got on hand (a Post-It, a hotel notepad, etc.). Writing the words down again makes the message more clear (since it's probably easier to read), and the act of rewriting the message also reinforces it further: a visceral connection to your wisdom.
- Now take that slip of paper — your own personal love note — and put it in your pocket or someplace on your person. I really do tuck my slip of paper into my bra strap on many days, because it's easy to access and I can feel the affirmation there against my skin.
- I recommend doing this in the morning so that during your day, you carry your affirmation with you as a tangible, loving reminder of your own wisdom.

Sources:
1. King, Joan C. (2009). *The Code of Authentic Living: Cellular Wisdom*. Word Keepers.

CHAPTER 5
Inner Affirmations: Bring on the Benefits!

"I can shake off everything as I write; my sorrows disappear, my courage is reborn."
—*Anne Frank*

PERSONALIZED AND AUTHENTIC

Now that you've been practicing non-dominant handwriting and pulling affirmations from the messages you've created, you might notice something shifting in your mindset.

With any mindfulness practice, the effects build up over time. What I love best about this mindfulness practice is that it is *truly personalized*. That might be one of the biggest benefits that it offers.

What does that mean, though? It's personalized because it came from listening to yourself. These affirmations are glimpses of your inner knowing and your deep-down truth. And now you carry that truth with you throughout your days, as a reminder of your wisdom.

You might note that some of the affirmations I post on social media and my website are about my experience with narcissistic abuse … but not all of them. For many months, after leaving the psychiatric unit, most of my affirmations were about healing from the abuse I endured.

Your self-affirmations are the result of whatever you're experiencing or need to process in that specific moment. These affirmations point to what makes *you* unique and special. They help you understand your inner desires and what makes up your core values.

I've been practicing this journal ritual for years now, collecting messages that I've saved as a reminder of my truth. And since I've recorded these messages, in a mindful and intentional way, I feel those things down to my core. I've tapped into who I truly am as a person.

I'm "living from the inside out," as Joan King puts it in *Cellular Wisdom*[1]. "You probably already know a great deal about what you most enjoy and feel comfortable doing," she writes. "But perhaps you've never taken the time to think about what these activities reveal about your coding and how you might harness the energy of your natural affinities to live more authentically from your core."

That's some really powerful stuff. Understanding our core values gives us more direction. Having these affirmations on hand has made me more confident, more empowered, and more connected as a person. Knowing what I want most out of life has helped me make clearer decisions and given me a more direct path toward the goals I set.

An example of this came shortly after starting my co-working business. Within a couple months of launching, I had filled the community space and was given the opportunity to expand within the building. I was terrified of increasing my expenses. What if I couldn't make it work? After a few days, **I chose to write about my fears**.

To put it simply, I was afraid of failing. Of being a failure in the eyes of my friends and family, not to mention myself. As I wrote, I knew it was the right choice to expand the business, and my fears were replaced with my strength and courage. I was committed and comfortable moving forward. I didn't look back and forged ahead (for the record, it was the right choice).

The benefit of using non-dominant handwriting as a mindfulness practice is that you're slowing down enough to **really listen** to what's written in your personal blueprint. That inner voice is powerful, if we just make time to hear what it's saying.

STRENGTHENING YOUR INNER VOICE

A huge benefit to the practice that you're developing here is that you're reinforcing your inner voice. Instead of shutting your affirmations away in a journal, you're writing these beautiful messages down again on a slip of paper.

And you carry those little nuggets of gold around with you all day — maybe even the next day, depending on the strength of your message.

This might seem like a small action, carrying around that little love note to yourself. But this little slip of paper is doing big work. It's reinforcing your truth. The slips of paper that I carry are proof of the work of self-love that I've been doing for myself.

The reinforcing part of this whole ritual is really important — and it's not a step that you should skip. I want you to really think of this piece of paper as a tangible representation of your truth. It's an authentic piece of who you really are, and this bold, clear truth bubbled up from the very depths of your being.

The small slip of paper honors your self-expression — I cherish these slips of paper and have boxes of them saved, to either share with others on my website and social media, or to carry around with me if the message rings true for me in that moment.

Small but mighty, these slips of paper carry truths that resonate with me and support my journey forward.

EVEN MORE BENEFITS

The benefits of this practice show up for me in all sorts of ways. Here are some other benefits that I've noticed when I keep up with this ritual of mine.

More Self-Efficacy

Self-efficacy is a concept that's been studied by behavioral psychologists for many years now, and was originally proposed[2] by psychologist Albert Bandura. Self-efficacy is having the personal belief that you can handle the challenges ahead of you. When you strengthen your self-efficacy, it builds a sense of empowerment within you. You learn to rely on your personal strength. You feel that to your core, and that starts to spill over into other areas of your life — everything from relationships to work to personal goals. Speaking of goals...

Better Goal Setting
Developing a habit, routine, or ritual (like journaling) reinforces the work you're doing in other areas of your life. Keeping up with your journaling practice cultivates your ability to focus, which lends a purposeful and aligned outlook to other aspects of your daily experience. This helps with goal setting, because the kind of consistency that daily journaling gives you starts to add up everywhere: You'll learn that you can rely on and trust in yourself, and that makes setting other goals feel a little less daunting.

Mental Health Maintenance
Personally, I've dug myself out of some very deep dark holes by using this practice. There's something so calming and rewarding around this ritual; it's probably no surprise that the practice of non-dominant journaling has become sacred to me. It's also been great for my brain. Sticking with a practice benefits your brain — knowing what to expect **feels good** to your neural circuits. According to Psychology Today[3], "The importance of routines has been associated with a variety of mental health conditions, including bi-polar disorder, addiction, depression, among others. The reason behind this is that when we organize ourselves and

know what to expect, it's easier to actively work towards counteracting the thoughts and symptoms of any of the aforementioned mental health conditions."

LAW OF INCREASING RETURNS

Spending your time in a mindful activity like non-dominant handwriting is an investment of sorts. I've been asked about the efficacy of non-dominant handwriting over time, if the benefits dwindle because your brain gets used to writing that way — or if my handwriting has gotten better after years of practicing this method. In my experience, my handwriting has not improved!

As for the time I've invested in this method, it has brought *increased returns* over time. I've used the method in so many places and situations*, not just during my mornings.

You'll start to cultivate some serious rewards when you stick with this practice. And I hope you do just that.

Don't worry, I talk about these places and situations more in Chapter 6.

EXERCISE

First, find a quiet spot and a guided meditation. You can choose one of my guided meditations on Insight Timer (always free) or one of the thousands of other meditations out there, on Insight Timer, other meditation sites, Spotify, YouTube, and so on.

Today, I want you to find a meditation on gratitude. Pull yourself away from the bustle of your daily routine, social media notifications, and back-to-back meetings. Quiet your mind and settle into a calm space.

Light some candles or incense if you want — there's no need to get fancy. The meditation experience should fill your awareness, and your environment should support that.

When the meditation ends, get out your journal. Sit in the feeling of calm that the meditation brought on for you, then start writing with your non-dominant hand. You can think through these questions if you need a prompt:

- What are you most grateful for in this moment?
- Where do you feel abundance in your life?
- How is your gratitude supporting you?

Were there any surprises?

Sources:
1. *King, Joan C. (2009). The Code of Authentic Living: Cellular Wisdom. Word Keepers.*
2. *Bandura, Albert. (2017). Self-Efficacy.*
3. *Plata, Mariana. (2018, October 4). The Power of Routines in Your Mental Health. Psychology Today.*

CHAPTER 6
How to Use This Writing Method for #AllTheThings

> "When you're writing, you're conjuring. It's a ritual, and you need to be brave and respectful and sometimes get out of the way of whatever it is that you're inviting into the room."
> —*Tom Waits*

#ALLTHETHINGS

I have my morning ritual of non-dominant handwriting, but really this journaling method works anytime you want to reflect on an idea, slow down your thoughts, or get some perspective.

Non-dominant journaling really does work for #allthethings. Maybe you're out running errands and just need a minute to get grounded. All you need is your journal and a quiet spot. I've used non-dominant handwriting in meetings and workshops, whenever I need to really connect with what is true for me.

And if you feel silly or embarrassed about the awkward display of your non-dominant writing, remember: this method is a practice of being both mindful **and more open-minded**.

When you start to use this practice throughout your daily routine, you're giving your brain a different way to process your thoughts. Each time you journal with your non-dominant hand, you experience something new — maybe a new way of feeling about things or a fresh perspective on a problem. But only if you're truly open to that kind of transformation.

That openness might make you feel vulnerable, but it also makes you smarter. According to Luke Smillie in *Scientific American*[1], "Open people tend to be intellectually curious, creative and imaginative. They are interested in art and are voracious consumers of music, books and other fruits of culture."

If you're like me, you enjoy learning and have a deep appreciation for information gathering. This practice of non-dominant handwriting is all about that. You're gathering and processing information in this practice — information that is coming from you.

Yes, it's about self-care and empowering yourself too. It's about staying open and truly listening to the wealth of information that you've gathered over your lifetime. Writing this way gives you access to that depth of knowledge and experience.

I'm excited to hear what you discover when you open those doors.

#ALLTHEPLACES

If you're the type of person who always has a notepad and pen on you, this practice is even easier. You'll start to find that any time you have a few extra minutes, you'll want to check in with your inner wisdom.

I've relied on this practice in the hospital, on airplanes, in hotels, and I sometimes practice non-dominant handwriting on my iPad when I'm traveling.

This method really is accessible and easy to use for a wide variety of occasions and in numerous settings. Even if you travel light, a journal and pen will fit inside a carry-on bag, and if you're like me and travel really light, you use your iPad and stylus for your journaling practice.

Soon, part of your packing-up or heading-out routines will include not only your keys and wallet, but also your notebook and pen.

#ALLTHETIME

It's an accessible practice because it really can work whenever you need it most.

When I went through the Narcissistic Abuse Survivor workshop, I found that I could use my practice of non-dominant handwriting for some of the exercises. The subject matter during the workshop was heavy stuff, and I needed to connect with what was really going on for me — especially during discussions that might be triggering.

It was helpful for me to have this writing practice to fall back on when parts of the workshop exposed some areas where I needed to do more processing.

This method works because I've started to see how it helps me process all kinds of situations or new information. By applying a mindful solution to life's daily stresses, we can start to build resilience and face new challenges with confidence.

And you can do that any time you need.

EXERCISE

This homework is a little different. Take a moment to think of times where you could use non-dominant handwriting to support you — between work meetings, in a waiting room, before an important conversation, during a workshop, after prayer. Make a list of those times and places (you might even make a list of opportunities using your non-dominant hand).

Soon you'll start finding even more reasons to journal this way, especially when you need the extra support. There are a few ways to stay consistent with this, so that you seize opportunities for journaling whenever they arise:

- Bring your journal and a pen with you everywhere you go. Get a pocket-sized notebook if you don't want to carry something larger around during the day.
- Find a quiet spot or corner (I've even used a bathroom stall in a pinch) to help you stay focused on the experience.
- Set an alarm if you need to keep an eye on time during an on-the-go writing session. Sometimes setting the timer for five minutes is all you need.

Sources:
1. *Smillie, Luke. (2017, August 15). Openness to Experience: The Gates of the Mind. Scientific American.*

CHAPTER 7
Inner Wisdom Encouragement

"Find out who you are, and do it on purpose."
—*Dolly Parton*

I'm thrilled that you're making non-dominant handwriting a part of your self-care practice. Once I started journaling this way regularly, I was able to nurse deep wounds and start some much needed healing.

I'm not fully healed, of course (are we ever?). I've continued to grow, and to rebuild my resilience, my trust of the Universe along with the people in it.

I know my journaling practice has helped me to manifest the support and love that I need. It's the scaffolding I've used to build the life I have today.

Today, I'm still healing, but I know that this healing has progressed, because I have my journal as proof.

My journal is a testament to how far I have come on my journey and the lessons I've learned along the way.

My journal is a symbol, in many ways, of my liberation.

MY HOPE FOR YOU

My hope for you is that this ritual helps to punctuate the routine of your day-to-day activities, instilling a balance and ease in your schedule that you'll start to rely on.

My hope is that you'll better cultivate the community and family that you need, especially since you'll start to trust yourself more. You'll be able to clearly ask for what you want or need from a place of authenticity.

And if doing this work has helped you, be an example to your friends. You'll start to see changes as you keep up with your Inner Affirmations, and this practice might be helpful for others. You might be able to find additional support (and accountability) for your practice this way. "Remind yourself that, as an adult, you can make choices to shape your family, to harmonize with your core values," writes Joan King in *Cellular Wisdom*[1].

I know now, after learning to trust my gut and my own inner wisdom, what fulfillment looks and feels like for me.

My sincere desire is that this book has done the same for you. At the very least, I hope the book gives you a self-care practice that you can fall back on when you need it most and when you need to reconnect with what you know to be true.

My hope is that you find limitless love for your own inner wisdom, wherever life takes you. Thank you for making me a part of that path.

For additional support, there is a Inner Affirmations companion journal to help with strengthening and supporting your new journaling ritual.

Share your affirmations with me online, using the hashtag #InnerAffirmations on social media!

THANKING YOURSELF

Before you grab your pen and start journaling again, I want you to take a moment to thank yourself for investing this time and energy into yourself.

Find a comfortable position, breathe deep, and **notice** your breath — each inhale and exhale.

And thank yourself.

You can access my breathe meditation if you would like to listen to that (it's on Insight Timer so it's always free). Or follow the meditation below:

Meditation
Taking the time to ground yourself with your breath
Allows us to move from our minds and thoughts into our bodies,
Allowing the two to connect.

Let our breath be calm,
And our mind will follow.

Pay attention to your breath.
Feel your breath moving in and out of your body.
Connect fully to the awareness of your body
By focusing on the sensation of your breath.

Take a slow deep breath.
And hold as you count to 5-4-3-2-1.
Release your breath slowly as you
Relax and release any tension within your body.

Let your your face relax,
Your shoulders soften,
Your fingers and toes soften,
As you let go of any stress.

Take another deep breath.
Hold for a count of 5-4-3-2-1.
Gently release your breath.

As you inhale again slowly,
Holding for 5-4-3-2-1,
Exhaling any remaining stress.

Breathe in calm,
Hold 5-4-3-2-1.
Breathe out any self-doubt or anxiety.

Breathe naturally.
Notice how your body feels, and if it feels differently than when you started.
Appreciating the calming power of your breath.

Thank yourself for this moment of self care,
As you reconnect with your inner peace, strength and wisdom.

Did you find this book helpful? Supportive? Inspiring? If so, tell your family and friends.
If you have a moment, I would be very grateful for you would leave a quick review of Inner Affirmations online.
Honest reviews help other readers discover their own Inner Affirmations!
Share your Inner Affirmation in social media and hashtag #inneraffirmations.
Or, better yet, share this book as a gift.

Sources:
1. King, Joan C. (2009). *The Code of Authentic Living: Cellular Wisdom.* Word Keepers.

CHAPTER 8
Resources For Your Mindfulness Journey

In this section, you will find some of the items mentioned, from books to workshops to meditations. You will find additional items that I have personally read or experienced and found helpful and enlightening. I only recommend tools, books, and services that I use or people I know personally. Integrity and authenticity are of the highest importance to me.

If you want to stay connected to my ever-changing resource list, you can visit the free Resources page on my website anytime.

BOOKS
I read every day. I usually have two or three books going at the same time (I'm sure that Amazon loves me).

The fiction I read in the evenings before bed to wind down my day.

The nonfiction is usually savored over a cuppa joe on a lazy Sunday morning.

Fiction
I enjoy a wide variety of genres: from murder mysteries like the Commissaire Adamsberg series, *The Three Evangelists*, and every Agatha Christie to historical fiction such as the Kopp Sisters series and even the nonsensical *Noir: A Novel*.

Nonfiction
The nonfiction I reads runs from self-care books like *Whole Again* and *The Passion Test* to more business-related subject matter with *Get Together* and *The 12-Week Year*, followed by more current topics such as *The Psychology of Pandemics*.

SELF-DISCOVERY

Brown, Brené. (2010). *The Gifts of Imperfection: Let Go of Who You Think You're Supposed to Be and Embrace Who You Are.* Hazelden Publishing.

Chödrön, Pema. (2020). *Welcoming the Unwelcome: Wholehearted Living in a Brokenhearted World.* Shambhala.

Christman, Christine. (2021). *Do You Want To Be Well? A Memoir of Spiritual Healing.* GoodWords.

Conner, Janet. (2009). *Writing Down Your Soul: How to Activate and Listen to the Extraordinary Voice Within.* Conari Press.

Gilbert, Elizabeth. (2015). *Big Magic: Creative Living Beyond Fear.* Penguin.

Hay, Louise. (1995). *You Can Heal Your Life.* Hay House.

Hicks, Esther, and Hicks, Jerry. (2004). *Ask and It Is Given: Learning to Manifest Your Desires.* Hay House.

Kawamura, Genki. (2019). *If Cats Disappeared from the World.* Flatiron Books.

King, Joan C. (2012). *The Code of Authentic Living: Cellular Wisdom.* Word Keepers.

Neustadt, Romi. (2016). *Get Over Your Damn Self: The No-BS Blueprint to Building A Life-Changing Business.* LiveFullOut Media.

Scott, Susan. (2004). *Fierce Conversations.* Berkley.

NARCISSISTIC ABUSE RECOVERY

Arabi, Shahida. (2016). *Your Brain on Love, Sex and the Narcissist: The Biochemical Bonds That Keep Us Addicted to Our Abusers.* Self-Care Haven.

Davenport, Barrie. (2016). *Signs of Emotional Abuse: How to Recognize the Patterns of Narcissism, Manipulation, and Control in Your Love Relationship.* CreateSpace.

Mirza, Debbie. (2017). *The Covert Passive Aggressive Narcissist: Recognizing the Traits and Finding Healing After Hidden Emotional and Psychological Abuse.* Debbie Mirza Coaching.

Northrup, Christiane. (2018). *Dodging Energy Vampires: An Empath's Guide to Evading Relationships That Drain You and Restoring Your Health and Power.* Hay House.

Resnick, Meredith. (2014). *Surviving the Narcissist: 30 Days of Recovery: Whether You're Loving, Leaving or Living With One.* BookBaby.

MEDITATIONS
Insight Timer

I was fortunate to find Insight Timer when I needed it most. I had struggled to meditate for years until I discovered the guided meditations here. Insight Timer is the world's largest free library of more than 90,000 guided meditations, 11,000 teachers, and the world's most loved meditation timer.

Since I was deep in the process of recovering from narcissistic abuse, I was looking for meditations that would guide me. I found some, but not many meditations that specifically covered the things I was dealing with at the time. That was when I decided to start creating my own. Since the beginning of 2019, I've created quite a library of meditations ranging from stress relief and Sleep support to narcissistic abuse recovery and self-empowerment. I branched out from my original purpose some time ago and found that I enjoy the creation — not to mention all the lovely messages I get from kind listeners.

There are plenty of other meditation apps, too.

Bethany Auriel-Hagan

I couldn't have asked for a better introduction to guided meditations. Bethany gave me hope, calm and guided me gently to be in the moment.

Some of my favorites:
- Awaken to a Clean Slate
- From Pain to Peace
- Becoming

Lisa A. Romano
Most of Lisa's tracks on Insight Timer are talks and discussions, along with her meditations geared toward narcissistic abuse recovery.

WORKSHOPS
Imago's Keeping the Love You Find Singles Workshop
According to the workshop's website, "Whether you're single, divorced, widowed or in a committed relationship our safe and supportive workshop provides the opportunity to explore yourself, uncover negative patterns and develop healthier and more successful relationships."

You can find a workshop near you with certified Imago therapists (the activities in this workshop are a perfect place to use non-dominant handwriting).

Melanie Tonia Evans
You'll note that some of the affirmations posted on my website and social media are around narcissistic abuse recovery — the combination of Melanie's work and my Inner Affirmations method helped to support me during some very dark times.

I stumbled across Melanie when I was at one of my lowest points. This expert on narcissistic abuse recovery, healer, author, and radio host provides healing methods that allow you to thrive. Her Narcissistic Abuse Recovery Program (NARP) walks you through the healing process to create an abuse-free life. Worth every penny.

ODDS AND ENDS
Writing Journal
I frequently get asked what I use to journal in daily. I've been using these plain, simple journals for years. I like the size, as they travel well, and the paper has a nice feel. This is what I give as gifts to friends when I encourage them to start journaling.

I also have my own branded journals available on my website.

Angel Blessings: Cards of Sacred Guidance & Inspiration
These cards were a gift many years ago, and I've always found them to be a great journaling prompt. I don't use them all the time, but on the days that I pull a card, I find the message or guidance to be perfect for my journaling that day.

BIBLIOGRAPHY

Introduction
Evans, Melanie Tonia. *Narcissistic Abuse Recovery Program.*
Insight Timer
Insight Timer - Katharine A. Chestnut

Chapter 1
Affirmations (New Age). (2021, May 10). In Wikipedia.
Wallace D. Wattles, (1910). *The Science of Getting Rich.* JonRose Publishing.
Rhonda Bryne, (2008). *The Secret.* Simon & Schuster.
Peden, A. R., Hall, L. A., Rayens, M. K., and Beebe, L. L. (2001). Preventing Depression in High-Risk College Women: A Report of an 18-Month Follow-Up. *Journal of American College Health*, 49(6): 299–306.
Creswell, J. D., Dutcher, J. M., Klein, W. M. P., Harris, P. R., and Levine, J. M. (2013). Self-Affirmation Improves Problem Solving under Stress. *PLOS One.*
Steimle, Josh. 7 Reasons Positive Affirmations Aren't Working for You.
Cuddy, Amy. (2015). *Presence.* Little, Brown Spark.

Chapter 2
Gut, Malgorzata, Urbanik, Andrzej, Forsberg, Lars, Binder, Marek, Rymarczyk, Krystyna, Sobiecka, Barbara, Kozub, Justyna, and Brabowska, Anna. (2007). *Brain Correlates of Right-Handedness. Acta Neurobiologiae Experimentalis*, 67(1): 43–51.
Does Writing By Hand Sharpen Your Creativity. Headspace.

Chapter 3

Marooney, Kimberly. (2010). *The Angel Blessings Kit, Revised Edition: Cards of Sacred Guidance and Inspiration.* Fair Winds Press.

Brown, Joshua, and Wong, Joel. (2017, June 6). How Gratitude Changes You and Your Brain. *Greater Good Magazine.*

Chapter 4

King, Joan C. (2009). *The Code of Authentic Living: Cellular Wisdom.* Word Keepers.

Chapter 5

King, Joan C. (2009). *The Code of Authentic Living: Cellular Wisdom.* Word Keepers.

Bandura, Albert. (2017). Self-Efficacy.

Plata, Mariana. (2018, October 4). The Power of Routines in Your Mental Health. *Psychology Today.*

Chapter 6

Smillie, Luke. (2017, August 15). Openness to Experience: The Gates of the Mind. *Scientific American.*

Chapter 7

King, Joan C. (2009). *The Code of Authentic Living: Cellular Wisdom.* Word Keepers.

ACKNOWLEDGEMENTS

I have been humbled by the outpouring of support by family and friends. Not just through the writing of this book, but through events I have experienced over many years. Some painful. Some not. In an effort to make sense of those experiences, I have learned how to care for myself in ways I would not have learned without their generous and unconditional loving support.

My thanks go to my parents for sharing their knowledge, vulnerability and taking me on enlightening experiences as a child.

My sister Lisa for encouraging me even though this isn't her 'kind of thing'.

A huge thanks to my beta readers. Your feedback and excitement have further validated my desire to share this with the world.

I especially want to offer my gratitude to the late Sue Myers of Breakthru Institute for introducing the method of non-dominate handwriting to me and certifying me as a Behavioral Kinesiologist.

ABOUT THE AUTHOR

Katharine Chestnut has an extensive and varied career background that spans many different industries. With a few decades of marketing experience under her belt, including a Diamond-level certification in trade-show marketing, she knows a thing or two about connecting with people in the business environment.

Katharine's love for connection and community is what drew her to small business culture. She transitioned from a global corporate environment to the world of coworking. She now plays dual roles as both founder and Chief Community Officer at Alkaloid Networks, a coworking space she founded in 2015. Katharine thrives on fostering connection for members who are growing their businesses. Additionally, she started the Atlanta Coworking Alliance nonprofit in 2019 to bring together local owners and operators in the region.

Opening a coworking space was a significant shift, and Katharine has mastered the art of adapting with grace, even while struggling through personal challenges. During the past two decades, she has navigated the realm of self-care, studying multiple wellness disciplines to support her own personal growth. She can shift seamlessly from marketing to kinesiology to coaching in the same conversation.

The culmination of her journey over the last few years is her most recent work, *Inner Affirmations*. This book is

Katharine's testament to her practice of self-care and the kind of growth that comes from a journaling routine. She is thrilled to share this transformative guide with anyone who might need its affirming support.

FIND ME IN #ALLTHEPLACES

Explore all the paths of personal transformation at
www.katharinechestnut.com.
Subscribe to my newsletter and get 2 free meditations.

Social
Facebook: KatharineChestnutAffirmations
Instagram: Katharine.Chestnut
LinkedIn: LNAL Life dba Katharine Chestnut
Pinterest: Katharine.Chestnut
Twitter: KatharineChest3
YouTube: Katharine Chestnut

Made in the USA
Las Vegas, NV
15 January 2022

41492917R00046